STORIES OF
WORK, LIFE &
THE BALANCE IN
BETWEEN

Tomson Robert

First published in 2016
Printed in India at: Repro India

ISBN 978-93-52016-97-6

Editing: Apoorva Tadepalli
Cover Design: Hirday Jayaraj

The Write Place
A Publishing Initiative by Crossword Bookstores Ltd.
Paradigm, A-Wing, 1st Floor, Mindspace, Link Road,
Malad West, Mumbai 400064, India.

Web: www.TheWritePlace.in
Facebook: TheWritePlace.in
Twitter: @WritePlacePub
Instagram: @WritePlacePub

Dedicated to Daddy – the one who demonstrated to me the meaning of integrity, dedication and hard work.

[P.S Mummy, I'll write another book dedicated to you]

ABOUT THE BOOK

Are you stuck in a job you don't love?

Are you made to do flunky work in office?

Do you struggle to balance work and life?

Do you want to quit your job and start a business of your own?

Do you wonder about the meaning of love and life?

If these questions apply to you, then this book is for you.

This book is a collection of 10 contemporary short stories based on the corporate world and life in general. Although these stories are a work of fiction, they capture real life situations and dilemmas that I have seen and faced.

Each story is aimed to leave the reader with a message. I believe these can help you answer the above questions. If not, I have tried my best to keep the stories as humorous and entertaining as possible.

ABOUT THE AUTHOR

Management Consultant by day and amateur author by night. Husband to a beautiful wife, father to an adorable baby girl and raised (along with a smart younger brother) by loving parents in God's Own Country (a.k.a Kerala, India).

Currently living in Dubai and working for a consulting firm.

Email: authortomson@gmail.com

TABLE OF CONTENTS

1

WHAT I LEARNED FROM MY FIRST JOB

"It doesn't matter what you have learned, what matters is your willingness to learn new things."

After struggling for 3 years to get into 'Guantanamo Bay', aka a top B-School, and another 2 years to stay in one, I finally managed to get my reward – a placement in an Investment Banking Firm that pays a 6 figure salary.

Like a Spartan dressed for war, I'm geared to conquer the 'Corporate Jungle'. My file, containing the sacred papers sanctified by my B-School seal, would be my shield. The innumerable hours of investment banking theories that my alma mater has imparted to me, are be my double-edged sword. With these I, David, the new intern at JW Associates, would fly my way into the C suite.

"Dave we're so proud of you. Can't believe my little boy is starting to go to office," Mom said.

"Thanks Ma. Dad can you please drop me to my office?"

"Sure Dave, give me 5 minutes to get ready," Dad said.

I reached JW Associates at 8 AM sharp, half an hour ahead of the scheduled time.

The receptionist escorted me into the conference room booked for the new interns joining that day. To my disappointment, a few of my fellow new interns were already there putting 'Amul' over Shilpa, the HR lady.

"Hello Ma'am, how are you today?" I said as I entered the room.

"No... No... In JW Associates there is no 'Sir' and 'Ma'am' culture," Shilpa said looking at all the interns gathered. "Each time anyone of you uses those *forbidden words*, you have to drop 100 Rupees into the Charity Box kept near the reception."

"Sorry Shilpa," I said.

"That's much better," she said.

As time went by, the remaining interns also joined us. We greeted each other with 'rehearsed pleasantries, fake compliments and lukewarm handshakes'. It was as though we were all chosen gladiators designated to fight each other, to death, to please the Emperor – Mr. Sharma - the Global Lead Partner of JW Associates.

Shilpa asked us to be seated and said that Mr. Sharma would be joining us soon.

Tie – check, suit – check, hair – check, breath – *check- failed*. I immediately swallowed a Mentos. This is the man who is going to determine my career; there is no way I'm going to screw up the first impression.

"Welcome to JW Associates," Mr. Sharma said. "From over 200 candidates interviewed, you have been handpicked by us to be the next generation of this prestigious company."

For the next 10 minutes, our Global Lead Partner gave *global gyan* that not only inspired us, but also reinforced our faith in the crumbing world economy.

Finally, Mr. Sharma ended his speech with a well enforced caveat in the corporate world.

"… and yes to help us achieve this goal, in exceptional cases you may need to put in some extra hours."

This was followed by a round of applause across the round table.

"Thank you Sharma *sir* for that inspiring speech," Shilpa said. Hope she deposits those 100 bucks in the Charity Box.

After the meeting, Shilpa assigned each of us to different Managers. I was assigned to a Senior Manager named Praveen Chandra, nicknamed PC.

"Hello Praveen, I'm David and I've been assigned to work with you," I said.

PC kept staring at his *PC* without the slightest acknowledgement of my presence.

I stood there for a whole 60 seconds before the guy looked up and said, "We have to attend a client meeting tomorrow, so I'll email you a report I drafted. Review the spelling and grammar and get it printed and bound. Ramu, the office boy, is on leave for a few weeks, so you'll have to do the printing and binding yourself."

I barely heard the words *'review the spelling and grammar'* and *'printing and binding'.* I only heard the words *'We have to attend a client meeting'.* I must be one of those lucky interns who get to face the client on the very second day of work. WOW.

I went back to my cubicle, all excited to get the work started. I found my fellow interns sitting nearby chitchatting. Jobless people, I thought to myself.

"Hey David, did you meet your Manager? Did he give you any work?" asked a beautiful intern.

I normally don't like to brag; however I could not resist this red apple.

"Yes I did meet PC. He asked me to prepare a report for a client meeting tomorrow," I said.

"*Arrewaah*, David is already on his way to become the best intern of our batch," another fellow intern said, trying extremely hard to hide his frown.

I didn't bother to respond. I had no time for these frivolous conversations.

It took me 3 hours to read the 100 plus page report. The language was pure blasphemy and required lot of rework.

Along with correcting the language, I also read the report thoroughly to get myself up to speed for the client meeting.

At 6 PM, I was ready with the printed report. But there was one problem.

The last time I bound something, I used a stapler. To my disappointment the binding machine wasn't a BIG STAPLER. How was I supposed to figure out how to operate this machine?

A chill ran down my spine. I could imagine the look on PC's face when he saw the unbound report; I could visualize him complaining to Mr. Sharma; I could picture the other interns laughing at me; I could see me not getting promoted; I could … STOP. Think David, think.

Although the B-School syllabus didn't include 'printing and binding', it had taught me 'where to look for information'. Thank God for Google and YouTube.

There are over 8 hundred thousand YouTube video results on 'How to bind a report'. Guess I'm not the first intern to search for this. Within an hour, I had watched 10 videos on the subject and was all set to bind.

My first attempt wasn't bad, but not perfect. Since I was determined to make an impression on PC, I was aiming for nirvana. I tore up the bound report and decided to give it another try.

The subsequent attempts were duds. The quality of my binding was decreasing with the increasing number of attempts (Economics happens to be a favorite subject). Mostly I punched the holes in the wrong places and whenever I got that right, the pages in the report were wrongly ordered. I should have stuck with my first attempt – my 'beginners luck'. Alas.

At 2 AM, I hit perfection. Bingo! What a feeling! Manual labor does give you some ecstasy.

I kept the report on PC's table and rushed home. As soon as I reached, I went straight to bed. I wanted to ensure that I was all fresh for the client meeting, the next day.

Same as the previous day, my dad dropped me to the office.

As I approached my cubicle, I could see PC in his cabin reading the report I had bound. I was a bit nervous on the feedback that I might get on my first paid work.

"So when is your client meeting?" asked the beautiful intern.

"It should be soon, PC is currently reviewing the report," I replied.

At 11 AM, PC got up from his seat, wore his coat and headed towards me. I also got up and wore my coat and was ready to leave with him for the meeting. I was super excited.

"I'm going for the client meeting. You needn't join. There are 2 printed reports on my table, bind them," he said with a straight face as he headed out the office.

I stood there numb. Maybe a small tear escaped my left eye.

"Why is PC not taking you to the client meeting?" asked the same intern who had christened me *'all set to be best intern'*. He must have got a sadistic pleasure from that.

That day, with my previous experience, I finished binding the reports faster. I wasn't asked to read the report this time, but I still did; I wanted to keep my mind busy and my senses away from my mocking counterparts.

This wasn't the end of my printing and binding journey. For the next few weeks PC made me print and bind atleast a dozen reports. To make matters worse, in the absence of the office boy, other managers also started giving me the same task.

This wasn't what I had slogged all these years in B-School for. Instead of writing of reports, I was merely printing them, instead of advising clients on mergers, I was merging papers. This isn't what I learned. I felt like a *glorified peon*.

One night, as I was staring into the darkness feeling miserable, Dad came to me.

"Dave, I've noticed that over the past few weeks something is bothering you. Is everything all right my son?"

"It's fine," I replied.

"You'll feel much better if you talk to someone," Dad said.

"And whom do I talk to? You? You're an old man who has no idea about the challenges we youngsters face in this ruthless corporate world," I shouted.

"Well then you should tell me. At least an old person like me can learn something new about the ways of the young," he said smiling.

I felt guilty for shouting at Dad.

"Dad, I'm sorry for raising my voice," I said.

For the next one hour, I told my miserable story to Dad. I cribbed and wept. Dad was right, I did feel better.

Dad listened to me patiently. I could see in his eyes that he genuinely understood my situation.

After I completed wiping my tears, Dad put his arms around me and started speaking.

"I was a 'nobody' in school," Dad said. "Average at studies, miserable at sports, zero at cultural activities and, to make matters worse, didn't have the looks that you got from your Mother."

"I think I got mom's brains too," I joked.

Dad smiled and continued.

"One day, when I was standing in the school assembly, I was randomly asked by a teacher to help out the school peon to setup the microphones and speakers for the assembly. I had to oblige. However soon I was the designated person for this job and had to do it every day. It took me a few weeks to learn the skill. Unlike today, microphones those days weren't cordless and speakers weren't light. Also you had to learn to control the 'bass' and 'treble' in the audio amplifier," Dad said.

I had no idea how all this was connected to my situation, but kept nodding as I didn't want to interrupt Dad.

"My friends nick named me 'Sound Operator'. I didn't like that at all. It was embarrassing and demeaning. My parents weren't sending me to school to be a 'Sound Operator'.

However as months passed, I realised that I was being called to all the functions in the school, be it sports day, cultural festival or even teachers meet, as all these required someone to setup the microphones and the speakers. This helped me to get acquainted with the teachers and even the Principal.

As time went by, my acquaintance with the teachers helped me to get additional responsibilities like - decorating the stage, charting the programmes and even making announcements. When I reached 12th standard, the teachers choose me as the 'School Sports and Cultural Captain'. I was selected for the post not because I was good at sports or cultural activities, but because I had seen and organised enough of them during my stint as the 'Sound Operator'."

"And that gave you the inspiration to start your own Event Management Company," I interrupted.

"Yes you're right," Dad said. "So what did you learn from this?"

"The guy with the microphone is always right?" I joked.

"That's rarely true," Dad said smiling. "But this is what the Sound Operator learned: 'It doesn't matter what you have learned, what matters is your willingness to learn new things'.

Maybe the B-School didn't teach you 'printing and binding', but it's a new skill, learn it. You'll never know, it may change your life."

We decided to call it a night, as I had to reach office early next day to do the mundane.

What Dad said did raise my inspiration meter, but it didn't last the night. The usual suspects - doubt and lack of patience - reined over me.

Office was deserted when I reached there at 7:30 AM. I went to my cubicle and started setting up the computer. Suddenly I heard a familiar voice from behind.

"Hello young man, do you by any chance know how to bind a report? The office boy is still on leave."

I looked back. It was Mr. Sharma.

Are you kidding? That's what your office pays me to do.

I took the report politely from him, bound it quickly and gave it back.

Mr. Sharma looked at the report and seemed impressed by my binding skills.

"Well done...what's your name?" He asked.

"David, I work as an intern here," I promptly replied.

"Good...so, are your investment banking skills as good as your binding skills?" Mr. Sharma asked.

I paused. This was my moment.

Imagine you are on *KaunBanegaCrorepati (Who Wants to be a Millionaire)* and the last question asked is something you have known your entire life.

As luck would have it, I had managed to glance the report that Mr. Sharma had given me to bind. The report was about an IT Company, and my miserable reading of PC's earlier reports had given me enough insight into the IT sector.

"Sir, I had a quick look at the report you gave for binding, I may be wrong but I believe the Current Ratio of the company we are recommending for our to buy is higher than the industry average. By looking at the Company's balance sheet, I believe this is due to the excess cash balance they have."

"Impressive David…very impressive. This was exactly my thought after reading the report," Mr. Sharma said. "I was looking for someone to help me with this assignment. Are you okay to work on this project? I can inform your Manager."

I smiled. I guess the glorified peon also learned what the Sound Operator did.

2

THE INTERVIEW

"Hard work without smart work is hardly smart."

I, Steve, was sitting in an 8 minute Group Discussion that started 5 minutes back. I'd not spoken a word till now.

It's assumed that the guy who speaks first in a group discussion and the guy who concludes, have a better chance of being selected. But in a GD group of 10, I am sure they will select more than 2 people.

The topic had something to do with subprime crisis in America. I carefully listened to what others said, as I knew BS (a.k.a Bullshit) about the topic.

Number 8, a pretty one, said that the crisis was a result of the housing bubble caused by the low interest rates offered by the US Federal Reserve. Number 6, said that the crisis was a result of something called Moral Hazard. Number 5, was throwing some weird jargons like Ninja loans, Credit Default Swaps and Blah.

Trust me; even if I was from Greece I would not know this stuff.

It was the 6th minute now. Everyone was trying to speak at the same time to make last moment contributions. The Moderator seemed least interested in controlling the group.

Now, it was my turn. I needed to get the groups attention, and I was in no mood to shout, like the others, to be heard.

And then my phone rang with a loud ringtone 'Who let the dogs out…'

Everyone looked at me.

I had asked my friend to call me exactly 6 minutes after I stepped into the GD. He had no sense of timing; he called after 6 minutes and 13 seconds.

Even before the moderator made any comment or I lost the attention of the participants, I cut the call and said, "Apologies for that… but let me ask you, is this a crisis caused by US Federal Reserve's low interest rate? Or is this due to Moral Hazard? I don't know. We can blame it on the Ninja loans and Credit Default Swaps, but what we are missing is that this is a crisis of lost trust, a crisis of lost morals and a crisis of lost hope. Let's try to focus on the human aspect of this crisis. In fact let's ask contestant 4, who has not spoken till now."

What I said was BS, but when you say it with a pinch of confidence, it's a sure hit.

Contestant 4 then took over and some other contestant concluded. I didn't care. Because I saw the look in the moderator's eyes, she was impressed. I am sure 3 points impressed her: one, I spoke about a new angle to the crisis - the human element; two - I asked a lot of questions, making other contestants think; and three - I gave an opportunity to a person who was silent.

The shortlist to the GD was out.

The contestant who spoke first, the contestant who spoke last, and I were shortlisted for the interview.

There were 2 other GDs also conducted by the Firm. Totally there were 9 shortlists, and all were competing for the one Management Consultant position at ACME, a Big 4 consulting firm.

We were all asked to wait in a conference room in the hotel where the GD was conducted. One by one candidates were being called into the interview room.

The candidates who completed the interview were not brought back to the conference room. They were free to leave.

I waited almost one hour, before I was called.

The interview panel consisted of four members. One of them was the moderator from the GD and she started the introductions.

"Hi Steve, my name is Shalini, I am a Partner at the ACME Bangalore office. These are my colleagues, Nandakumar, who is a Partner at our Chennai Office, Pratyush, who is a Manager in the Bangalore office, and Ram, who is a Senior Manager in the Kochi Office."

"Hello, nice meeting you all," I said.

"Please Steve, have a seat," Ram said.

"So, Steve, we have seen your CV, however, it would be good if you can give a brief introduction about yourself," Shalini asked.

This is the same BS question; everyone has to answer, in every interview, no matter which part of the world.

Being from a Tier 3 B-School and doing an internship in an unknown consulting firm, I had zero chance of getting the job in this big league consulting firm. So, I was going to play the underdog, because everyone loves an underdog.

"Respected panel, to be frank, I know that you have seen my CV and noticed that I don't have an Ivy League degree or a prestigious internship to get this job." I paused to analyse the reaction of the panel. I seemed to have caught their attention, so I continued.

"Till six months ago, I was a guy without any ambition, one in the crowd, invisible to my lecturers, and a disappointment to my parents. I was mediocre.

However one day, I attended a career guidance seminar in which a leading Partner from your firm was giving a speech. His speech really motivated me."

"Do you know the name of that Partner?" Shalini asked interrupting me.

I looked at Nandakumar and smiled.

"Me?" he asked, surprised.

"Yes sir, you. I had come down to meet my cousin studying in Chennai Loyola College and I happened to hear your lecture there,' I said. 'I was motivated by everything you said, especially the part on – anything less than extraordinary is a waste of time…"

"…so live an extraordinary life," Nandakumar and me said in tandem.

The truth is I never went to that lecture and in fact I was not even anywhere near Chennai that time. When I was doing some online research on the key Partners in the firm, an article popped up detailing the speech given by Nandakumar.

"Sir, that is the day I decided to have some ambition in life, that is the day I started to dream," I said. "Since you explained how exciting Management Consulting was, I decided to take it up as a profession."

Nandakumar seemed to have touched the roof. I am sure he felt good being praised in front of other colleagues in the firm.

"That's great Steve, we are happy to hear that," Shalini said. "But tell us why ACME? Is it because Nan, that's what we call Nandakumar, is from this firm?"

"Well, Nan did inspire me to have an ambition and try out Management Consulting, but, I must apologise that I did do an independent due diligence of which is the best Management Consulting firm, and as per my research BWC and ACME topped the list," I said and gave an intentional pause.

"Then why choose ACME?" asked Pratyush. This was the exact question I wanted to be asked.

"Well, I applied to both BWC and ACME, but BWC didn't call me for an interview," I said.

All the panel members laughed. Bingo. I was glad to know that I was playing my pipe well.

"I was surprised to see a profile like yours shortlisted for this position, given that you are not from an Ivy League college," Pratyush said.

"Well, I really wanted this job, so through LinkedIn, I got in touch with your HR head, Namrita. I told her my story and begged her for a chance and she, being kind hearted, decided to give me one," I said.

It was not as easy as how I said it. Convincing Namrita was a pain. I emailed her like a hundred times before she responded. Then I constantly followed up with my 'Underdog Story'.

I think she let me through the selection process, thinking that I wouldn't stop bugging her until she did. Well, she was right.

"So Steve, this is a consulting job and involves solving lot of problems. To test your problem solving skills, I am going to ask you a puzzle. It's not difficult and you should be able to solve it easily," Ram said.

Shit, I suck at solving puzzles. I didn't know how I would outsmart my way through this one.

"Imagine you have 3 bags with you, one with yellow toys, one with red toys and one with a mix of toys with both the colours. The colour labels on all the three bags are wrong. What is the minimum number of draws you would need to make, in order to identify which bag has which colour toy?" Ram asked.

I had no clue of the answer. I am sure the question was simple. But whenever I hear a puzzle, my mind somehow goes blank. Think Steve, think.

"Steve, you seem lost. Do you want us to repeat the question," asked Shalini.

I stared to sweat a bit. But suddenly I got an idea. My Dad used to tell me – honesty is the best policy.

"Ram, I am not going to answer this question," I said.

Ram was surprised.

"Why is that Steve? Aren't you even going to try?"

"I don't need to try, I have heard and solved this question before." I paused. "I know what the answer is."

"So you know the answer is two times," Ram asked.

Ram seemed to be a shrewd guy. As he asked 'if I knew the answer is two' I felt something different in his tone and mannerism. Is this a trick?

"Ram I told you I know the answer, why are you testing me again," I said putting on a fake smile.

"That's very honest of you Steve. I really appreciate that," Nan said.

"Steve, what's your expectation from the ACME?" asked Shalini.

Honestly Aunty, I would like ACME to pay me a million dollars, for hardly working. But I can't blurt the truth out. I had to give a very diplomatic answer.

"I would like ACME to provide me with exposure to various clients and industries, so that I can learn and disseminate the knowledge that I gain from it," I said.

The Aunty was impressed.

The panel continued asking various questions. Some technical and a few to test my attitude. I outsmarted most of the questions.

"Well Steve, it's been a pleasure talking to you," Shalini said. "We will take a day or two to announce the interview results. You can give our HR a call after 2 days."

I had to end this with some BS.

"Thank you all. No matter what happens, it's been a pleasure and I learned a lot," I said. "Nan, it was great meeting you in person."

I was sure I had cracked this interview. If not, BWC's interview was a week later. That 'not getting the interview call' part... I lied. It was not just Namrita, ACME's HR, whom I had chased.

3

'TIME' FOR WORK LIFE BALANCE

"Work life balance is a matter of priority. Even God rested on the 7th Day"

"…and Ben we've to send this presentation to Boss first thing Monday morning," John, our company's Senior VP, said to me, his minion, as he left office.

The presentation was an interesting one and was as exciting as it could get in a bank's back office; however when you hear *'first thing Monday morning'* at Friday 10 PM, it can only mean that your weekend is ruined.

Now I've to tell Rahul, my minion, that he would've to postpone that much awaited, 12th, *'girl meeting ceremony'* in his hometown by another week. His mom arranges these marriage proposals every alternative week and Rahul ends up judiciously cancelling most of them citing work reasons. But this time he was counting on going and hopefully, finalising. He'd actually shown me the photo of the girl he was going to meet. She was pretty. Unfortunately, given the economics of the marriage industry, if Rahul did not see her this weekend and close the deal, she's a Gone Girl.

I'll just have to ask Rahul to blame it on John-ism. That's the term that Rahul had invented for the mannerisms of John.

John, my boss, had a reputation for overcommitting and conveniently delegating to his subordinates to deliver. On a typical day, my team and I would execute our routine bread winning tasks, and when the time came to leave office, a slimy voice from behind would ask –

'You guys leaving? Half day?'

'Is there anything urgent John?' I'd ask.

'We've to send a very important report to HO tomorrow morning and I need urgent help.'

I have no clue how more work always comes up at 6 PM in the evening.

This had become a weekly routine and slowly John was baptising us into his kingdom of servitude. Last month, two of my team mates, Priya and James, quit citing work life balance issues.

I headed back to where Rahul was sitting to break the news.

'Rahul, John wants the presentation by Monday...' I said reluctantly.

'NOOOOOOOOO,' shouted Rahul. The empty office echoed his voice and also the emotions of a desperate bachelor.

'I was really looking forward to meeting this girl,' he said.

I felt sorry for the guy.

'Okay, let's stretch tonight and cover as much ground as possible. You can leave tomorrow early morning. I'll pick up the rest.'

Rahul was relieved to hear that.

'Are you sure Ben?' He asked hesitantly.

I nodded with a smile.

'Thanks a lot Ben. If this marriage proposal works out, you know who my best man is.'

'Thanks man,' I said.

I explained to Rahul what needed to be done and we went back to our respective cubicles to start work.

I texted my wife. No reply.

I popped a Red Bull, loosened my tie, rolled up my sleeves and peered into the bright screen in front of me.

Hours went by. Before I knew it, 3 cans of Red Bull and 3 AM had passed us by. Sometimes, keeping busy at work helps you bury your problems, atleast for a few hours – not sure if it's a good or a bad thing.

I looked at Rahul. He'd dozed off on his current better half – the company laptop.

'Dude wake up…let's call it a night…err…or maybe a very early morning' I said waking Rahul up. 'Email me your work and *pack up*.'

'Pack up' – that's my favorite word – Pack up, go out and get a life.

'Let's have a coffee and leave, Rahul, I can't let you drive with such drowsy eyes,' I said as we headed out of office.

We went to the *New* Irani Tea stall located outside our office. The shop has been in the area for the last 10 years and I'm not sure why it's still called '*New*'. Anyway, it's open from the wee hours and serves strong tea and fresh onion samosas for miserable office souls like me.

We ordered the usual and sat outside the stall.

'Hey Rahul…sorry for the grind,' I said.

'Ben, it's not your fault…just blame it on *John-ism*,' Rahul said smiling.

He paused for some time and said, 'Sir you've elevated through the corporate ladder so fast. In just 3 years, you've made it from a mere Executive to Senior Manager. I want to have a career like yours. What's the secret?'

I was in no mood to give career advice at 4 AM. But given the fact that this guy would be married soon, I felt obliged to tell him not to make the same mistakes as mine.

'The secret is simple. It's where you allocate the most important resource in life.'

'What's that?'

'Time.'

Rahul stared at me for an explanation.

'We all have limited time in this life; we've the option to invest this time with our family, with our friends, in our hobbies or even in our career,' I said. 'Unfortunately I chose to take *time* out of other priorities and invest in my career. The investment did pay off, and that's what is seen in my fast growth…but it was not without a price.'

I don't know if what I told was too much for a 26 year old bachelor to comprehend.

I looked away, took a deep breath and stared into the flame heating the tea pot. Then I looked straight into Rahul's eyes and said, 'What I mean Rahul is that you should definitely focus on your career, but it shouldn't be at the cost of time spent with your family, with friends or your hobbies. It's okay to wait an extra year or two to get that promotion and not get boggled with fast tracking or climbing the ever greasy pole called the Corporate Ladder.'

A long silence and then Rahul reacted.

Rahul's reaction to what I said bordered between an acknowledging smile and a *'You've been there and done that, but don't want others to try'* smirk.

We finished our tea and headed to the office basement. I wished Rahul that this be his last *'girl meeting ceremony'*.

After Rahul left, I went to my car, opened the trunk and took out the spare clothes I'd brought from my *broken* home and went back to the office to finish the presentation.

4

LIMITED BY DIMENSIONS

"It is difficult to say what is impossible, for the dream of yesterday
is the hope of today and the reality of tomorrow"

"Does God exist?" I asked my favourite teacher.

She smiled.

"David, this is a question that man has asked ever since he existed. Although the questions is real, the search for the answer has always been limited by dimensions," She said.

"What do you mean by that?" I asked.

"Before I tell you what limited by dimensions means, did you know that in 1992, Pope John Paul II apologised to Italian scientist and philosopher, Galileo, who in 1633 was sentenced to indefinite imprisonment for merely suggesting that the planet Earth revolved around the sun?

With our access to telescopes and photographs of the planetary systems, the theory suggested by Galileo is a well-known fact today. However the scholars in the 17th century did not have access to these and were reaching conclusions about Galileo's suggestion based on their limited knowledge at that point in time," she said.

"I didn't know that. But how is it related to existence to God? Even with all the technology we have today, we have not been able to conclusively prove the existence of God," I said.

"That is true. But you too are making the fundamental mistake that the scholars in Galileo's time made," She said.

"What is that?" I asked.

"You are reaching conclusions on matters, based on your limited knowledge at this point in time without considering future possibilities. Let me give you another example of this. In 1895, Lord Kelvin, the President of the Royal Society of England said that 'Heavier than air flying machines are impossible'. But you and I know that this 'impossible' was made possible by the Wright brothers in 1903," she said.

"Hmmm. Interesting," I said.

"Now let me tell you what limited by dimensions means. You know that there are three dimensions we can see- length, width and height. Now imagine if your eyes could only see and understand two dimensions – length and height. How will a cube look like to you?"

"If I cannot see the width of the cube, I will only see it as a square that has length and height. It will be a 2D image than a 3D," I said.

"Exactly. In the same way - God is an equation that we cannot see or understand with our limited three dimensions, just like you will never be able to understand what a cube is if you only understand two dimensions – length and height.

"As we humans mature and learn to access more dimensions, it will get us closer to solving this equation," she said. "Today most evolutionary biologists dismiss God as the creator of the universe based on the 'chicken and egg' example. Again a classic example of reaching conclusions within our limited knowledge, at a point in time."

"Are there more dimensions than length, width and height?" I asked.

"Well, Einstein believed that Time is the 4th dimension and someday in future we can travel through time. This seems impossible with our limited knowledge at this point in time, but this may be a fact tomorrow," she said.

I was a bit overwhelmed to hear all this. But since I had watched the movie *Interstellar*, some of this made sense.

"So David, the question if God exists, still remains. But the important thing is to keep the search on. As Robert H. Goddard, the inventor who is credited with creating and building the world's first liquid fuelled rocket once said – 'It is difficult to say what is impossible, for the dream of yesterday is the hope of today and the reality of tomorrow'," my favourite teacher said.

5

THE NOT SO SOCIAL NETWORK

"We are part of a generation that 'Looks Down' – it's time to look up and network in the real world."

5:00 AM

Buzz Buzz.

It was another stupid WhatsApp message. I know I should just ignore it. It'd be one of the guys, from one of my many WhatsApp groups, saying 'good morning' or forwarding a picture on the same lines.

But I can't resist the temptation. I, Steve, suffer from what physiologists call no-mobile-phone phobia a.k.a. Nomophobia. The symptoms of this include constantly checking the phone for notifications or feeling lost when separated from it. A chronic symptom of Nomophobia is having illusions that your phone is ringing or vibrating, when actually it isn't.

I checked the message. It was one of those stupid messages which ended with 'If you don't forward this message to 10 people in next 10 minutes then…'

I diligently forwarded the message to a WhatsApp group which had more than 10 people. I hope that counts.

6:20 AM

I woke up to my iPhone marimba alarm tone. For the past 20 minutes I'd been putting it on snooze.

While getting up, I checked my phone for any notifications. Thanks to my real time checking, throughout the night, there were none.

I can't spend an hour without checking my Facebook feeds. I don't post or share, but I checkout everything. I'm what people call a 'Stalker'. If my friends (or even 2nd degree connection strangers, without a good privacy setting) could see who viewed their profile, I'd be among the top 5.

Another thing—my source of NEWS is Facebook. With the real time feed, I am way…way… ahead of The Times.

8:00 AM

Three of us were in the kitchen having breakfast.

As I poured milk into my bowl, I checked Facebook again.

The milk spilled. Shit.

I looked at Neha, my wife. She too was glued. Her mouth was chewing the whole grain bread and her brain was chewing whatever she was reading on her iPhone.

My two year old son, Arya, was playing with the Tom Cat App. Because of this App, every conversation we had in our house, echoed.

Arya's first word, ever, was something like 'Buzzzz'. When he was six months old, he hated it when Neha or I used to talk on the phone. He'd start crying. I guess with age he started embracing technology.

As I left home, my wife said, 'Hey I need the car today, I've to meet the girls for brunch. We're making a 'Selfie' calendar to raise funds for children in Africa.'

'Ok dear,' I muttered. Last year the 'girls' were all about ice and rice buckets, this time it's the 'selfie' calendar. Gone are the days when they were happy with Oprah and Silly Grewal.

9:00 AM

I took a taxi to the office.

Throughout the journey, the driver was on his phone and I could hear one side of a husband-wife fight over the usual suspects—the in-laws.

I got a picture on my 'P haters Group'. P stands for 'Pratyush', my Boss. The picture was from Sid. He used an App to blend Pratyush's face with a Zombie's. Frankly, I didn't find much difference. The group christened Pratyush 'Zombie'.

My phone battery was low. Thankfully I had back-up power.

Got a text from my wife that today was James' birthday. Susan, James' wife, and she were planning a surprise at 6:00 PM. I don't like James, he's horizontally challenged and anti-Apple. No wonder 'keeping the doctor away' isn't working for him.

Tonight, Arya will be with his grandparents. Wonder how they'd put him to sleep without those YouTube videos.

11:00 AM

Zombie called for an emergency meeting to discuss the dropping client satisfaction ratings for ACME, our firm. I was checking Facebook while waiting in the meeting room. Not too many updates. Payal had put a photo of her dead dog. Not sure it was appropriate to like, although the post had received 50 likes.

As I was checking out the dead dog's photo, I heard a voice from behind - 'Steve is there something happening inside your pants, you seem to be staring down intensely.' It was Zombie.

Everyone had a good laugh. Embarrassing.

1:00 PM

The meeting was a disaster.

Zombie mentioned in the meeting that our new Partner, Anu Pillay, will be joining ACME next week. I spent an hour checking her profile on LinkedIn. As per LinkedIn, she and I have no skills and expertise in common. I wondered how we would get along.

My wife had uploaded selfies from the brunch. 73 likes in just 10 minutes. I'm sure if I don't like and comment, dinner's going to be cold for the week.

2:00 PM

I was hungry and decided to go to the ground floor to grab lunch. At the 12th floor, a guy entered the lift and pressed 10th floor. When the lift reached the 10th floor, he was busy playing Candy Crush. I didn't want to disturb.

5:45 PM

Reached James' house. The front door was open, so I walked in.

There were 3 of us. Neha and Susan had arranged everything perfectly—great decoration, amazing cake and a much needed gift—a treadmill.

There was some chit chat for some time, and then we all started staring at our respective phones.

When I finished checking more photos of Payal and her dead dog, and looked up, I saw James. He was staring at us. Shit, I should have closed that front door.

"Sup…ri…se," I shouted. Others followed with a dying tone.

9:00 PM

The surprise was a well-deserved flop with a capital F.

I was happy to reach my flat. I wanted to chat with this new Facebook friend I'd made. He lived in Tokelau, a territory of New Zealand in the South Pacific Ocean. It's really awesome how technology connects people around the world.

In our flat's corridor, there was a really tall man standing.

"Hello may I help you?" Neha asked.

"I am fine, thank you," he replied smiling.

"What are you doing in our corridor" I asked trying to be all manly.

"I'm your neighbor, Mr. Sharma," He replied. "I've been living here for the past 5 years."

Neha and I just ignored him and went inside our well networked lives.

6

HOW YOU BECAME A HORRIBLE BOSS

"When the buck stops with you – Do something about it"

John, my boss, is a pain in the ass. He just dumps all the work on me and expects me to complete it like – yesterday.

He has a different level of sadism and I hate him to the core.

He says that I take too many vacations when my last vacation to Greece was before the crisis. He makes me feel like leaving office at 7 PM is a half day. He calls me on Saturdays and gives me work due on Monday.

Today I lost it on him.

I had told him that it was my new girlfriend's birthday and needed to leave by 7 PM. But still, at sharp 7 PM, just when I was about to leave, I saw an email in my inbox. It was from John, requesting me to complete a report, which was due next week, tonight.

I lost it. His sadism was getting too much to handle.

"How can you dump this work on me when you knew that I had to leave early for my girlfriend's birthday?" I shouted as I furiously opened his cabin door.

I expected him to be shocked, but the guy just sat on his black leather throne, undisturbed and unaffected with the melodrama I was creating.

"Ben, I need that work done. If you can't do it, I will call Rahul and get it done."

Rahul, the newly and hopefully happily married guy, had left the office half hour back. This jerk actually has the audacity to think that he could call Rahul and get the work done that was not even due for another week.

"Sir…How you became such a horrible boss?" I blurted in angst.

He smirked.

"Well I can assure you that it did not happen overnight. It took years of training - being bullied, screwed over and treated like shit - for me to be reach this state of pure bliss.

"I started as an intern, right at the bottom of the greasy corporate ladder. When I joined the bank I knew that it was no Hogwarts. There were no magical wands, but just whips, that too in the hands of my seniors. To fast track my career, my servitude to the organisation was 24 x 7 – be it 3 AM or Friday night.

"Apart from the flunky work my seniors made me do, I was christened the 'go-to' person for any stationery requirements, given the honor to fetch coffee and snacks and make dinner and lunch reservations. However, I didn't complain, I kept my head low and persevered, because of which I was promoted to the next level.

"At the next level, the butchery was not physical, but emotional. Every good work I did and every great idea I had, did not belong to me. Forget appreciation, I considered myself lucky if I was CC'd in the email where my boss was claiming credit for work submitted by me. But you know what, when it came to mistakes, I got the full credit – for both mine and my boss's.

"But I persevered for the sake of my career. I have had losses in this journey…"

John paused his monologue. I knew that like me, John too was divorced.

John drank some water and continued. "…I have had losses in this journey – a bit of health issues, a bit more of personal issues and a lot of character issues. But I had no time to live in the land of regrets. I swallowed my tears and the little ego I had left, and rolled with the punches.

In time, I did not just survive, but became one of the youngest and most successful managers in this company. And Ben, all that experience just made me the person I am today – in your words - a horrible Boss."

I felt sad for the guy. I guess he had too much going on inside.

"Sir, I am sorry to hear that. But now that the buck stops with you, you can make a difference," I said, "If you continue to treat your juniors the way you were treated, they will also end up…" I bit my tongue.

"…becoming a 'Horrible boss' like me?" John completed my sentence.

"I didn't mean that. I meant that it will be just another vicious cycle," I said.

John thought for a bit.

"Ok, Ben you can finish the work tomorrow. Please go and have fun with your girlfriend. Hopefully this one works out for you," he said smiling.

I was very happy to hear that. I was afraid that my outburst would ultimately hit back at me.

"Thank you sir. And I am sorry if I was rude. I was just…,"

"It's okay, Ben. I understand," John said.

I immediately switched off my laptop, packed my bag and rushed towards the parking lot.

As I was nearing the parking lot my phone buzzed. It was a message from Rahul and it read – *Sir, that jerk John is asking me to do a report tonight. I believe that report is not even due until next week. John-ism I say.*

7

WHAT IS LOVE?

"The Eagles were right about what they sang about Love"

"Do you love me?" was the message on my WhatsApp. I'm sure by now the two blue ticks have appeared on the other end.

Ann and I had been dating for the past two years. Like in most cases, a mutual friend introduced us. It didn't take us long to get from movies with friends to movies with just us. We clicked well – from not liking dogs to keeping a blog, from our interest in movies to conversations on how that's sabotaged by crying babies, and from our inability to cook to inexcusable addiction to Facebook.

My phone buzzed again. "It's ok Dave, you don't have to reply. GN."

I wanted to reply, but I wasn't sure.

Two years of dating a guy, is a long time for any girl to wait to hear that she is loved. It's not like in the past I've not said it to any girl. But all those ended in a bad way and this time …this time I didn't want to make the same mistake.

As I lay on my bed staring at the empty ceiling, I prayed for some wisdom. But all I got was heavier eyelids. I resisted sleep and kept thinking…

Suddenly, I saw myself in a different place. To be exact, inside what looked like a shop. As I looked around I noticed that it was a fruit shop.

"Hey pass me some fruits of 'Care'," said the lady standing at the counter.

The lady looked like she was in her mid-thirties. She was dressed like an ancient Greek woman.

"Dave, are you dreaming?" she asked.

When I heard the word 'Dreaming', I realised that I had slept off and this was all a dream. Usually, in a dream, when I realise that I'm dreaming, I wake up. But this time I didn't. It was be one of those rare occasions when you have the luxury of continuing to dream, even after you know that it's a dream. I decided to help the lady out.

"Can you please tell me where exactly it is?" I asked.

"It's on the second rack towards your right. The 'Care' fruit has an olive green colour with RGB – 146, 208, 80," she said.

I realised that RGB stood for Red, Green and Blue, which are the primary colours and from which, all other colours are derived. I spotted the second rack and from the labels, identified the required RGB or the 'Care' fruit.

As the lady said, the fruit looked olive green. But I wasn't sure why the fruit was called 'Care'. There were also other fruits on the rack with different variations of the green colour. On the opposite side, there was another rack; it contained fruits having various shades of red.

"Please pass that quickly," she said. "And after that please pass me some fruits of 'Anger'; it's on the rack opposite to you, bright red with RGB – 254, 0, 0."

There were lot of customers waiting in queue at the counter and the lady kept requesting me for one fruit after the other. Although I struggled initially within a few minutes I was able to service her better.

After some hours, the lady indicated to the customers that she was going to close the shop for an hour for lunch.

"You hungry?" she asked me.

"Yes I am, but I don't want any fruits," I said smiling. I was never a big fan of fruits.

She smiled and said, "Here in Utopia, we've only fruits to eat. Try them, the green ones are bitter, but the red ones are really tasty."

"What are these fruits and why are they named after emotions like 'Care' and 'Anger'?" I asked.

"Well the answer is in your question itself. These fruits are from the Tree of Knowledge and eating them adds emotions to your life. So when you eat the fruit of 'Care' you start to be more caring and eating the fruit of 'Anger' makes you a really angry person." She said.

Wow. This means that, in Utopia, you literally become what you eat.

"Are all these fruits produced from the same Tree of Knowledge?" I asked.

"Yes all these fruits are produced from the same tree. Good emotions, like 'Care', 'Happiness', 'Sharing' etc., come in various shades of green and bad emotions like 'Anger', 'Jealously', 'Pride' etc., come in shades of red," She said. "We use the combinations of RGB to distinguish each shade of green and red."

"Oh I see… but why would someone eat a fruit of a bad emotion… say 'Anger'?" I asked.

"As I'd mentioned earlier, the green ones, although they are good for you, are bitter. However the red ones are very tasty. So although people in Utopia know that the red coloured fruits are bad, they still eat them,"

That made a lot of sense. It's like soft drinks and French Fries, we consume them, even though we know they're not good for us.

I looked around the shop; there were so many fruits – both green and red – the green ones included 'Happiness', 'Caring', 'Sacrifice', 'Patience', 'Friendship', 'Kindness', 'Joy', 'Trust' and many more. The red ones included – 'Anger', 'Jealousy', 'Selfishness', 'Fear', 'Disgust' and 'Sadness'. But there was something missing.

"Where is the fruit of 'Love'?" I asked.

"What is 'Love'?"

"You don't know 'Love'? It's the best feeling in the world and it's what life is all about," I said. "I'm sure if it was a fruit, it will be the best fruit ever."

"That's interesting. I'm not sure why such a precious emotion isn't produced by the Tree of Knowledge," she said. "Have you ever experienced this emotion called 'Love'?"

"Of course yes, I've been loved by my mother, my father, my sister, by Ann…" I bit my tongue.

"Well I've a way to understand what this emotion is," she said. "Come with me."

She took me to the lawn outside the shop and made me sit on a chair. She sat opposite to me, and gave a tiny blue berry to eat.

"This is a called a dream berry. Dream of a person from whom you've experienced this emotion called 'Love'. As you dream, I will hold your hand and it will help me identify the corresponding RGB of the emotion," she said.

"I'm already in a dream, how can I have another dream?" I asked.

"Haven't you seen the movie Inception?" she asked smiling. "Let's try it out, just for fun."

I closed my eyes and decided to dream of Ann. Soon I was asleep.

There were many instances that flashed before my eyes. The way Ann smiled the first time we met, how she took care of me when I was sick, the times she would lend me money when I was broke, all the times she laughed at my pathetic jokes, how she organised the surprise birthday party for me, how, despite hating cooking, she made me my favourite chocolate brownie, and how she is always the first to forgive, when we fight.

I woke up from my dream within a dream.

"Aha I know what this 'Love' is," the Utopian lady said.

"What is it?" I asked.

"Well when you were sick, Ann used the fruit of 'Care'. When you were broke, Ann used the fruit of 'Share'. When she laughed at your stupid jokes or organised your birthday or made brownies, she used the fruit of 'Nice'; every time you guys fought she used the fruit of 'Patience'. So you see, she's been eating a lot of green fruits, even though they are bitter.

In Utopia, this emotion you refer to as 'Love' is known as Equilibrium. Equilibrium happens when you've a balanced diet of all green fruits," she said.

Ann does love me, I know that. But am I in 'Love' or 'Equilibrium' with her? Even if I am, how can I be sure that our love will remain in the future?

As I thought of these, I realised that I was waking up from my dream.

"Thank you for telling me all this," I said. "Before I wake up, may I know your name?" I asked the Utopian lady.

"My father named me after a feeling that Equilibrium or 'Love' hangs on to," she said.

"What is that?" I asked.

"Hope."

8

TO BE OR NOT TO BE AN ENTREPRENEUR

"It's true – fail to plan means plan to fail."

"I quit," I said to Anu Pillay, the new Partner at ACME and my new boss, and it felt damn good.

This is the day I stop working for someone and start working for myself, a day I'll give up office tension and take up my passion, a day that I die as an employee and be reborn as an entrepreneur...

"Why do you want to quit Steve?" asked Anu.

"I want to be an entrepreneur and follow my passion," I said.

"That's amazing Steve, good choice," Anu said smiling. "Let me know when you want your last date to be."

Is that it? I came to Anu's cabin expecting to be cajoled not to leave the job. Instead she was encouraging me to leave. I know everyone is replaceable, but some persuasion would've been nice.

"Err...I would like to leave after serving my notice." I said.

"Excellent...please send me a formal resignation and I shall take it up with HR immediately."

"Okay Anu…" I said.

Anu resumed her work, as I remained in her cabin confused. I didn't think that it was going to be this easy. I'd come prepared for a speech on entrepreneurship and following one's passion, but it was now all gone in vain.

As I stood lost in my thoughts Anu asked, "Steve, is there anything else?"

I was curious and wanted to ask why she was being so cool about my resignation. This was different from the usual Anu I'd seen. I thought I was one of her best employees.

Then I gave into my curiosity.

"Anu, why are you not trying to stop me? I'm sure that I'm not that bad of an employee," I said.

Anu stopped her work, looked at me and said smiling "Because I know you've made up your mind and if I say something to stop you, you'll give me THE SPEECH."

Both of us laughed. "How do you know I'd prepared a speech?" I asked.

"I too was an entrepreneur," she said. "I too had quit my job for it."

"What happened with that?" I asked. I'm sure if Anu had a promising business she wouldn't be doing this job.

"Let me guess, you want to start a restaurant right?" Anu asked.

I was surprised how she got that right. "Yes…"

"Well three out of five budding entrepreneurs want to start a restaurant. Even I did," Anu said. "However I was so blinded by passion and impulse that I forgot the fundamentals – doing thorough research and having a business plan. The only experience I had with a restaurant was eating from one. I'd no clue about what happens inside the kitchen and the operations of a restaurant. Within the first month of opening the restaurant, I was slapped with a fine from the local authorities for not meeting certain safety standards. I also ran out of working capital within the first quarter."

What Anu said, resonated with my current situation. A couple of my friends and I got the inspiration to start something on our own after attending a seminar on entrepreneurship. It was an impulsive decision. The closest we had to a business plan were notes scribbled on a tissue paper.

I became nervous. Shit, I should not have taken such an impulsive decision.

"Steve, don't worry. I wanted to tell you this at the beginning itself, but you wouldn't listen if I forced it on you. I reacted the way I did, so that you would start a conversation and seek advice," Anu said reading my face. "Now, can I have that report on our competitor, JW Associates, which I asked you for yesterday?"

"Yeah sure," I said, a bit confused. "What about the resignation?"

"What resignation?"

I decided to stick to my job, do my homework and get the fundamentals right before I follow my passion.

9

WHAT'S YOUR AMBITION IN LIFE?

"Love what you do, even if you are not doing what you love."

During Performance Appraisal, I asked this question to my best employee, Jane. Her answer was perfect. I wish, I'd known the answer to this 'Question' the way she did.

This is a question that transcends through your life, right from a tender age, when life is full of possibilities and neither your education nor physical state limits the prospect of you pursuing your ambition.

Guesstimates indicate that, at an age of five, eight out of ten boys would answer the question as 'to become a pilot'. Mine was no different. At five, the motivation to this was definitely not the airhostess. It must've had something to do with the aura and the style the pilots carried, with their cool caps, uniforms, aviator watches and, of course, the shades.

However this ambition of mine was broken when, in high school, I was forced to choose Commerce as my major, instead of Science.

Nevertheless, if one ambition is broken, a young soul can always pick another.

In high school, forming a 'Boy Band' was my ambition. Obviously Backstreet Boys, Boyzone and of course the girls, were the major motivators. My friends and I even formed a high school boy band. We bought cool T shirts, sweatshirts, shades, 2nd and 3rd hand instruments, and even made a poster for ourselves.

However we couldn't make it, because, frankly none of us knew how to properly play the instruments, and worse, to sing.

By the time I reached college, I was no longer the master of my own ambition. The truth is, like many of us, I was confused. My choices were vastly influenced by what my friends wanted to do, what my parents said and what my uncles, aunties, relatives and even the neighbour suggested. The options were plenty – Lawyer, Auditor, Investment Banker, Hotel Management and many more. And like how we get confused with the number of options of tooth brushes in a super market and finally make a random choice, I chose to be an Investment Banker, and enrolled myself for the Chartered Financial Analyst (CFA) course.

Little did I know about the Herculean difficulty of the course. Years went by, and I just managed to complete half of it. However, with this qualification, I managed to a get a job in a multinational bank.

What I do in the bank, cannot be told in two lines, so I'll save it for another day, but I assure you, it's far from anything great.

So here I am, 30 years after the age I wanted to become a pilot. Stuck in a back office job, with a fancy title. To my merit, in just 3 years, I've made it from a mere Executive to a Senior Manager. But I come to office day in and day out, do the business as usual - mange my team, my customers and my bosses. I have no clue why I do this.

I hate my job and lately, I suck at it. I started making silly and unforgivable mistakes. My Boss, John, surprisingly has been patient, however I am not sure when it will drain out.

The main reason for me hating my job is that, I still carry regret. Every time, while flying at 30,000 feet, when I hear "Ladies and gentlemen this is your Captain speaking..." – a sense of regret fills my heart, drowning me with thoughts of missed opportunities consisting of 'ifs' and 'buts'. It suffocates me.

I'm not doing what I love and worse, I don't know what I love doing. I've no ambition and am just going with the flow.

'What's your ambition in life?' – If someone asks me, as they still do, I struggle and just blabber.

However Jane had an answer.

When asked the question, her reply was "My ambition is to love what I'm currently doing, because I really don't know what I love to do. This way, I'll be good at what I'm doing and in the meantime, I can find what I love to do."

It took a while for my half CFA qualified brain to process this answer.

Seeing my confused face, Jane quickly asked me a question back: "Ben, which subject did you score the highest in school?""

"English, I loved that subject. I scored the maximum in it," I said.

"And which is the subject you hated the most?"

"Science," I said.

"So here's a guess – Among other subjects, I am sure you've scored the lowest in Science. I am right?"

I smiled. Low score in Science was the reason why I was forced to take Commerce, instead of Science, in high school.

"Yes your guess is right." I said.

"It's an old lesson that my tuition teacher taught me, if you try loving the subject you are studying, no matter how much your brain hates it, eventually you will do well in it," Jane said. "When I lost my husband, I only got this job with my work experience. I don't exactly love this work, but I make a conscious effort to try and love what I am doing. In that way I can be good at it and can sustain my family."

"No wonder you are the highest rated employee in our team," I said.

"Thanks Ben, but loving what I'm doing also gives me a hope that someday when I know what it is I want to do in life, I have the time and the means for it."

It was a simple lesson. One which is obvious and everyone knows inside, but chooses not to think about.

I thanked Jane. Knowingly or unknowingly she had helped me.

We all need to make ends meet, Jane being a single mom and me being a parent, have responsibilities. Living with the regret of lost opportunities and confusion of ambition, eat up our present, which ultimately is the building block of our future. Doing well, right here and now, is the answer. This will sustain us and, in the future, provide us with the luxury of pursuing what we love.

So I decided to love what I'm doing, even if I'm not doing what I love. That's my ambition. The rest will just have to fall in place.

10

MIDNIGHT CONVERSATION WITH SANTA

"The fundamental principle is - don't stop having fun – be it work, life or the balance in between."

I have this habit of getting up in the middle of the night and drinking water. Thanks to the lights on our Christmas tree, I was able to navigate easily towards the fridge. As I opened the fridge, temptation stuck me in form of Minced Pie. I decided to treat myself with a slice.

I sat on the dinner table to savour my midnight snack.

Suddenly, I sensed a shadow moving near the Christmas tree. I became nervous, as there have been instances of robbery in the neighbourhood in the recent past.

Then, I heard a noise from behind.

It said – "Ho…Ho…Ho."

I fainted.

When I opened my eyes, there was an old man in front of me - with long white hair and a white beard. He wore a round spectacles and had a red coat on.

"Who are you and what are you doing in my house?" I asked.

"Don't you know me Dave?" He asked. No one called me Dave, other than my parents, Ann and a Utopian lady.

I stared at the old man. He looked very familiar. I had seen this guy somewhere before.

Shit – I know who this guy is – no way, it can't be him.

"Are you him?" I asked.

"Yep, I am him," he said.

"There is no chimney in my house, so how did you get in?" the sceptic in me asked.

"I will never fit in a chimney," The old man said smiling and pointing to his tummy. "I just used the door. You see, over the years, I have mastered the art of 'breaking in'. It's convenient and keeps my clothes clean."

"Makes sense." I said "And what about the deer?"

"Rudolph and his gang are parked next to the empty spot near your car park," he said. "Hope no one will come there soon."

"Don't worry, that family has gone on holidays."

"Ho – Ho – Ho, I love going on holidays. Although December is my favourite month, I can never take leaves during the month. You see, it's the busiest month for me," he said with a wink. "All the other months, I just have to supervise the elves making the gifts. But in December I have to deliver them."

"Do you still make the gifts? You can save a lot of money by outsourcing them to a sweatshop in the East," I said.

"Ho – Ho – Ho, that's funny. We are modernising with the times, but some things are best kept classic," He said. "Speaking about gifts, don't you want your gift?"

"I think I am a bit old to receive gifts," I said.

"Gifts are fun, and you are never too old to have fun," he said. He put his hand into his red bag, took a tiny gift wrapped box and gave it to me.

I must confess – I was a bit excited to receive the gift.

"Go ahead, open it," he said.

I quickly opened it. It was the shiny round marble that I had found during my childhood days in our backyard. I carried it everywhere I went – it was my lucky charm. As I touched it, it unlocked infinite memories of my childhood - the smell of the rains, the old town parades, cricket matches in the open plains, and of course the food my Mom made. The marble was like a pen drive of memories filled with fun.

"It's all coming back, ha, just like that lady Celine Dion said," he said with a smile.

"Thank you, I don't remember how I lost this," I said.

"You lost it the day you stopped having fun," he said.

"What does that mean?" I asked.

"I found this in your house, it was lying right in front of you always – on your work table. But you never saw it because you stopped having fun and decided to be like any other adult – running the rat race towards success defined by someone else. You decided to grow up and kill your curious nature, you decided to fit into the cliché and stop asking questions because it may be 'stupid'."

"That's too deep," I said.

"I know – Ho - Ho - Ho," he said. "But Dave, look at this marble, remember the memories it stores – don't let go of it, don't stop having fun."

I was feeling a bit irritated with all this preaching - I hated being preached to.

"Like you said, you work once a month buddy, but I have to work 24x7 for 365 days to make ends meet. There are no elves to help me out," I blurted out and regretted it the next second.

"Dave, just don't stop having fun," he said smiling. "Remember the child in you."

My alarm rang. I woke up from my sleep. Although it was Christmas day, I had to send out some reports to my boss - Mr. Sharma.

I quickly started working, conveniently ignoring the shiny round marble on my work table.

The End

www.ingramcontent.com/pod-product-compliance
Lightning Source LLC
Chambersburg PA
CBHW020607030426
42337CB00013B/1256